For Rylynn & Makaylee & Brady,

Best Wishes & Happy Reading!

♡ Sarah Barnard

Francesca

By SARAH H. BARNARD

Illustrated by Katherine Bourdon

Applewood Press

MMXVI

Published by Applewood Press, Muskegon, MI 49441

ISBN: 0997959304
ISBN-13: 978-0997959307

Printed in the U.S.A.
First Edition, 2016

FOR JACOB & SALLY

This one's for you, Mom and Dad,
whose unconditional love and encouragement
provided a comfortable base for discovering and spreading my wings.
Big bear hugs up to you both! ♥

Special Acknowledgements
Thank you: Laura Hayes, Josh Bourdon, Diane Walkowski, Elizabeth Prentice
Steve Barnard and Craig Bourdon

In her own little world,
a home beautiful and sound,

There sat a spoiled pup
on a soft, puffy mound.

Her name was

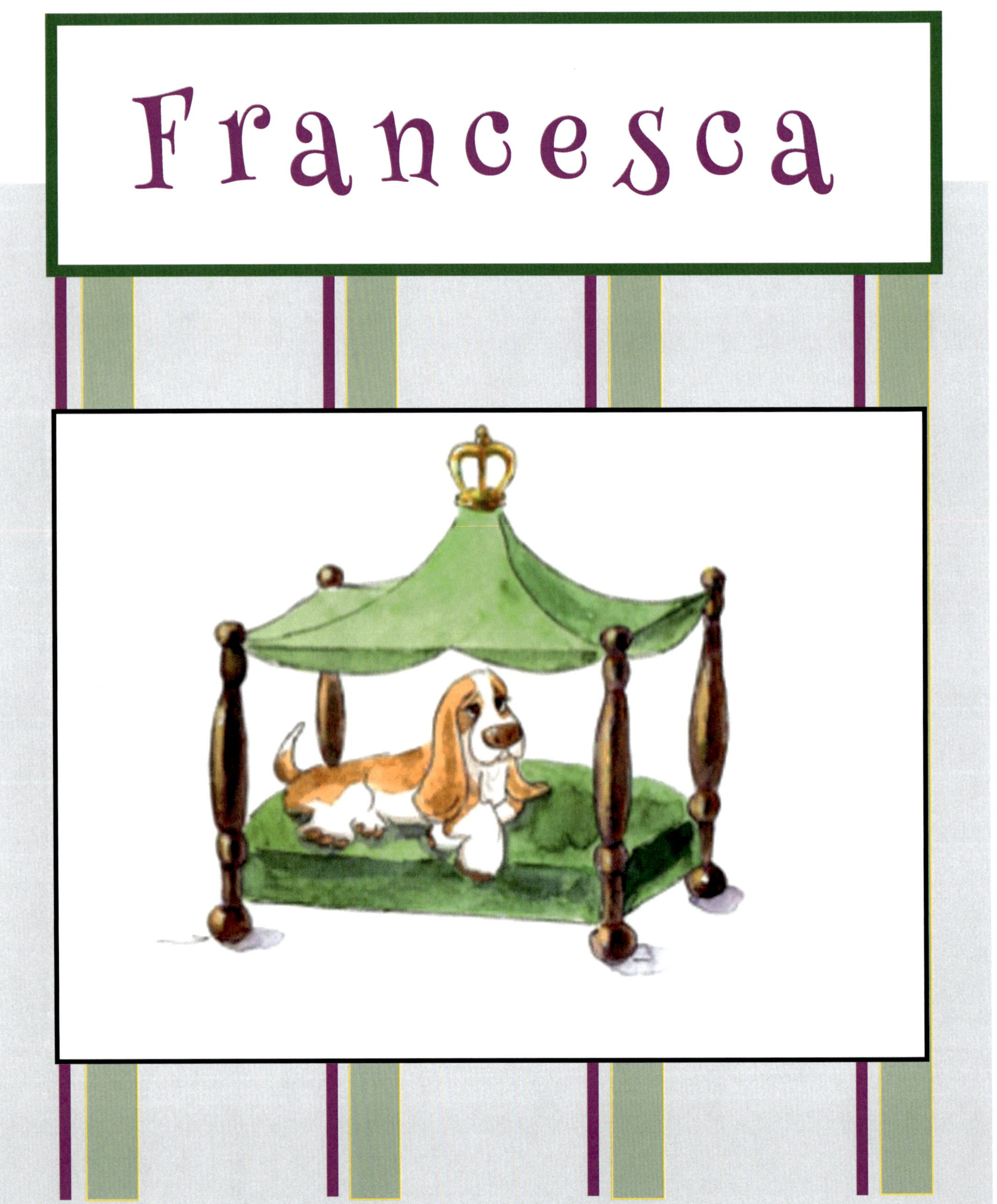

And as one might guess

Her looks were astonishing;

yet her thoughts

... quite a mess.

Her soft, beautiful fur

was pristine and luxurious -

Silky brown blends -

so, it made her quite furious . . .

When those dirty,

pesky insects

tried hitching

a ride

On her long

beautiful ears

or her tender

backside.

So

furious,

in fact,

she *never*

resented

the tub

Where

Annie

lathered

her gently

and would

carefully

scrub.

She

desired

a fine coat

no matter

what it

would take.

And always

thanked

her sweet

Annie

...with a

showering

shake!

But

all was not

sunshine in

Francesca's

charmed

life.

For

there was

something

she craved,

and it gave

her great

strife.

Weeks

upon

weeks,

it

corroded her

mind,

And

there

seemed

no solution -

no obvious

kind.

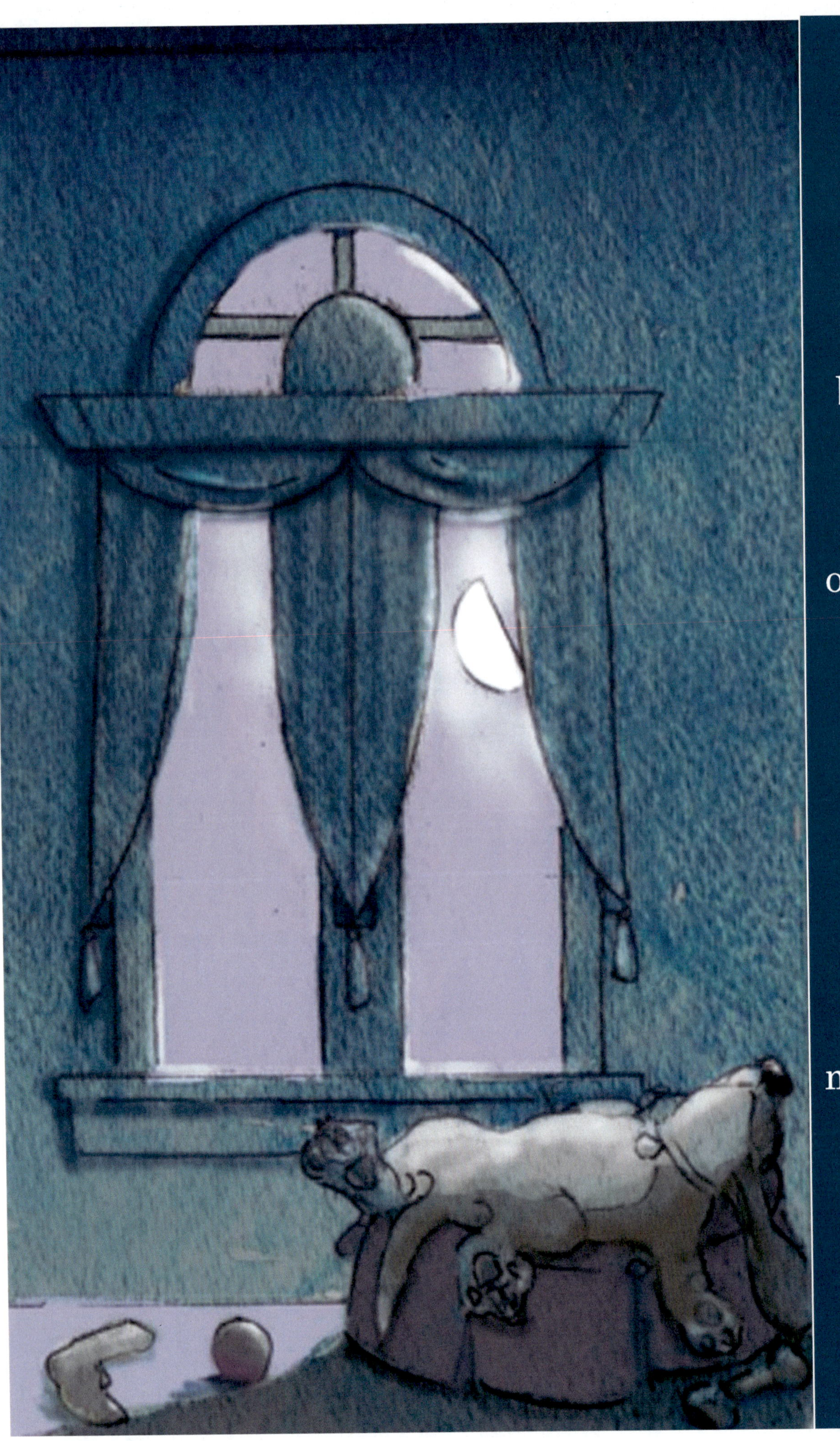

What

could

possibly

be remiss

for this

one special

dog,

Who

received

more kisses

than the

fairy tale

frog?

Well, a curious discovery revealed what was lacking.
Outside, wagged a friendly beast, filthy and hacking!

And
though
scary
and
icky
this
curious
sight,

Gave her
warm
loving
feelings
night
after
long
night.

Until the day she and Annie
walked side-by-bike to the park,
Where Fran's toys lay buried
under sand, grass and bark.

When, lo and behold,
she spied 'the beast' in the trees!
Its fur muddy and matted
and harboring fleas.

Francesca sneered at the sight.
Yuck! Had she been insane?
But, Annie ran straight to him
with no sign of disdain.

Then Annie gasped, and whispered,

"You poor little thing!"

Seeing his shriveled hind legs

her tears started to sting..

She knew that those legs

had never moved - not a wiggle

Then, the dog started kissing her,

making her giggle!

Through happier tears, Annie snuggled this stray.

We'll call you Lucky," she managed to say.

Lucky wagged, then barked, so desperate to play -

but jealous, Francesca growled and wandered away.

She found it amusing Annie called this dog "Lucky."

He was dirty and hungry… and he smelled *really* yucky!

and really challenged her mind
Was how he trotted on two legs -
the others dragged behind.

They left scraggly lines where the dirt ran thick

She carefully placed Lucky in the basket on her bike,

Brought him home, bathed him,
and fed him all he would like.

Francesca resented Lucky's bath
but she *really* had her fill
Of his cart, lovingly made,
from *her* human's goodwill.

Annie had worked day and night,
hammering nails into wood.
Then spent more hours making
it as lovely as she could.

Then, Annie shrugged and said,

"Time to try this thing out!"

She placed Lucky inside it

and let out a shout:

"Go on you two!

Show me how friends can play!"

Lucky quickly took off,

swerving every which way!

In time, Lucky maneuvered

every tricky turn and jerk

With wheels crafted to replace

legs unable to work.

And Francesca grew certain,

beyond any slight doubt,

That she, too, needed a cart,

Annie *must* figure this out.

But the sweet lovely girl,

unable to read her dog's mind,

Did not know Francesca's thoughts

were so jealous and unkind.

Poor Annie thought her dog
settled near Lucky to bray
Because she loved him so dearly
or wanted to play.

Really, Francesca was puzzled:
could she be friends with a mutt?
But as she watched his love for Annie
she grew out of this rut.

She put a stop to her envy—

for this 'mutt' was really ...FUN!

And suddenly her soul became lighter

as if warmed by the sun!

And as Lucky got filthy,

Francesca gave it a whirl,

For both enjoyed time

with their favorite girl.

And bath time had become

an extra-sneaky fun treat

With two dogs in a bubbly tub

splashing Annie's bare feet.

Soon,

those two

were the

very

best

of friends

Once

Francesca

stopped

resenting

the cart

on Lucky's

end,

That rickety, worn cart

made by Annie's loving hands,

Which often got stuck

in the deep playground sands.

And when it did,

Francesca would lend him a paw,

Then they would run side-by-side

chasing after the ball

That was thrown by the girl,

much, much wiser than she ...

Who understood

the deep value

In friendships of three.

ABOUT THE AUTHOR

Sarah, age 4 with Heidi

Sarah Barnard was born and raised on the beautiful shores of Lake Michigan. She currently lives in Muskegon, Michigan with her husband, Steve, and their sweet rescued mutt, Maya – who's nearly as pampered as Francesca! Her early love of reading and creative writing paved the way for her to earn a Bachelor of Science degree in Elementary Education, and serve her well in her job as the media clerk at a local elementary library. In her off hours she is often creating images as a professional photographer. Sarah is thankful she and her siblings, Annie and Jay, were raised with silly basset hounds, like Francesca. She is also thankful for her husband, their three incredible daughters, and homemade chocolate chip cookies, for being there to help her through the hard times and celebrate the great times.

ABOUT THE ILLUSTRATOR

Kate, age 7 with Tinker

Katherine Bourdon is a native of West Michigan living in Muskegon. She taught vocal music in public and private schools in Michigan for more than 30 years and retired before pursuing her other passion in art. Katherine's artwork has received numerous awards throughout the years from exhibitions at the Krasl Art Center in St. Joseph, MI, the Muskegon Museum of Art, The Kalamazoo Institute of Arts and the Michigan Regional Arts Exhibition at the UICA in Grand Rapids. Her artwork has been purchased by private collectors in the Midwest and Canada, and has been acquired and displayed in several corporations, hotels and financial institutions throughout Michigan. To see more of her amazing work, visit http://www.katherinebourdon.com.

Made in the USA
Columbia, SC
17 June 2017